FUNDAMENTALS OF STARTING A BUSINESS

In The Era Of Technology

By Shivansh Bhanwariva

I0479742

[TOC] Table Of Contents……………………

- *Team Work*
- *Execution*
- *Action Plan*
- *Innovative Product/Service*
- *Courage To Bear The Tall Poppy Syndrome*
- *Hiring And Firing*
- *Adaption To Changes*

How To Scale A Business?.......

- *Collaboration*
- *Provide Free Value Forever*
- *Care For Your Customers*
- *Show Up To Customers*
- *Chase The Attention*
- *Change The Intent*
- *Winning Marketing*
- *Speed up the process*
- *Disrupt The Industry*

How To Manage A Scaling Business?.......

- *Treat Your Employees*
- *Control Your Expenses*
- *Find Partners And Enable Crowdfunding*

An Advice To Sustain A Business.......

Introduction

Starting a business is one of the most important decisions to be made in life. The reason being is that it is something that lets you live the living standard you have always dreamed or thought of. It gives you the real freedom of being a boss and control the world around yourself. From the perspective of luck, you have won the biggest lottery of this universe, which is, you are a human being on earth. If you are not driven and fired up and willing to sit like a lump to wait until you die without doing or having the thing you always wanted to do or have, life goes on the darkened stage.

There is no significance of getting an opportunity to be a creature on this blue planet if you don't build the business of your dreams or be the person you have wanted to be. Keeping in mind all the obstacles, challenges, ups and downs, and fundamentals, this book will give you a better understanding of what a business actually is, what it takes to start and build a successful business in the evolving world of technology, and finally, how to sustain or manage that business by playing the long-term game in the today's corporate world. Besides that, you will also learn the underlying ideology behind creating a vast business empire without having to worry about any form of politics and insecurity.

What Is A Business – A Short Explanation

The theoretical definition of a business that everyone can access is very impractical. Business for most of the people is buying and selling something as a way of earning money. But that is not what it really is. Taking a step further, let us practically define a business.

It is a repeatable process of creating something that brings value that other people need at a price that they are willing to pay. It is all about meeting the expectations of the consumers and making their life more accessible than ever before. But this notion is always ignored by the far majority of people while starting or running their own. Still, it is a subjective definition you may or may not want to consider and agree with.

A business is looked differently by different eyes. From the perspective of an employee, a business simply means a way to reside a fulfilling life. For a person with a spark to change the world through innovations, it can just be a way to connect with people at their convenience. For someone belonging to a low-income family or section, it can mean a high-income source. A busy executive might think of it to be an opportunity to work on what he wants to, not on something he is supposed to or has to. But one belief remains the same throughout every circumstance and place, which is, a business is not a job, and it can't be learned in schools and universities. It is never organized and neat, like the rows in your classroom or the writing styles in your copies. Schools and universities never teach you a thing about business. What they train you for is being a robot who follows orders of the seniors and nothing else.

They teach you that your job is to get a job which is very conservative and safe. You work nine to five, have lunch in between, get back home, struggle with your financial goals, get upset, and finally, go to bed thinking you have to do a lot of work the next day. This process goes on for months, but that is not the case with business.

There is nothing organized and expected. One day you may go very high and another day very low. But that is what makes it different from all other major models of earning money and living life. If said in a straightforward sentence, a business is no different from life. It is because life also has various good and bad moments. When you get to face a disease like diabetes, it will never knock the door of your room and ask whether to come in or not. It just happens. The same story goes with running a business.

You can't just start a business because you are bored with the current job, or you want to flex a Ferrari to other people in your circle. There is something even deep to be taken into account before starting any venture. It is one of the most challenging things to be done practically.

Why? Because there is a lot of value to be brought upfront on the table.

So, when you are nobody, a business is defined as a lot of judgment, negative reinforcement, underestimation, insult, and taunts.

Fortunately, all of that is temporary. Once you figure out your thing and start getting results, it becomes your hobby and irresistible passion.

Jeff Bezos – the founder of Amazon, says that you can't be proud of your talent, but you can be proud of your choices. It is because you choose to work hard and take the pain for the gain of running something big that ordinary people don't think about. You choose to be creative and different from others.

That is what it is all about - making an impacting difference.

"A business has to be involving, it has to be fun, and it has to exercise your creative instincts." – Richard Branson

What Does It Take To Start A Business?

Many of us think it is only the money that is needed to start a business, but that is not more than a myth and misconception. Besides capital, there are other essential things or 'factors' involved in the process. Yes, it is a long process. Let us look at what it exactly takes to start a business.

Investment

An investment holds a very vital position in starting a business. If you don't want to spend money on something, you are not much serious about it for sure. Here, the term investment refers to both time and money. Giving a lot of money and not time will most likely hurt you and vice versa. No matter what you think about the world to be, it is exactly going to be what it is going to be with or without the way you thought it is going to be. Nothing great is going to happen with magic if you don't invest the required time and money. Suppose you decide to run an online business of selling hoodies; you will have to give some money to someone for making that online presence to get in front of the targeted consumers. But that is just a small example of creating an endowment.

You might have an idea to start the next Google, Netflix, or Microsoft, but not having the courage to take the money out of the pocket for that one initial stage will never allow you to make new steps further. But investment should always be made after homework. With no clear concepts, strategy, and understanding, investment of both money and time can lead to severe unexpected results in a negative way. Separation of emotions from your objectives makes the venture profitable.

You have to invest in the right things at the right time strategically for long-term revenue generation.

Now, there can be one more case - you may not have the money with you to start. For this, the perfect solution is - OPM! OPM refers to Other People's Money. If you don't have the money, you go about taking it from other people around on some claims of returning. In today's world, it is generally known as a loan. Many successful entrepreneurs like Robert Kiyosaki and others had started their businesses with the help of loans. You can't just sit on the bed and hope for money to come. Either you raise it through funding, or go about loans for your right investment.

"I will tell you how to become rich. Close the doors. Be fearful when others are greedy. Be greedy when others are fearful." – Warren Buffet

Audacity

Are you willing to take the risk? Every day in business is full of uncertainties. Some are too big to be considered, and others are not. But still, it always has the eye-opening moments. You need to decide if you have that pain tolerance. There have been two kinds of people in this world - ones who take the risk and others who regret their whole life. When considering the instance of football, some players get hurt a little bit and sit down with the excuse, whereas some break their back and play until they fall unconsciously. That is what happens in business.

If you are good enough to build the most significant business in the world, if you are good enough to be at the top, nobody is stopping you from being there. The only thing that stops you is your willingness to take risks. There is no safe game to be played in a business. There is no value of your emotions because what matters more than anything is the customer and their feelings. When you get deep down inside the core, you will notice everything becoming so clumsy and messed up. You will worry that you have not done enough yet.

It will be like the most shuffled puzzle to solve, and that is the real feeling of success — either risk or regret. Everybody among your loved ones can pick up two, three, four things very quickly that they regret. And right now, they feel okay because they have got a lot of life to go. But when you spend time with someone in their eighties and nineties, the thing you will absolutely figure out if you really dig is regret. People, in the end, don't be proud of them playing it safe. They don't talk about what they did but talk about what they wish they did.

The certainty is when you are ninety, tired, not mobile, and it is over, you can't do it anymore. You can't build the company you wanted. You can't spend that time with your kid. You can't drive the car you dreamed of in your childhood. That is regret. Hence, you need to take the risk to take one step backward for two steps forward in your life. If you have that audacity, it can literally change the world around you.

"I could either watch it happen or be a part of it." – Elon Musk

Sacrifices

When you ponder about business, what basically you are thinking is a dream. And dreams require sacrifices.

Everybody talks about what is not working. The hard and unacceptable truth is that everything is working the way it used to, only the one who is not working is you. Ultimately, you make things happen.

People look at Bill Gates, Warren Buffet, Mark Zuckerberg, and Elon Musk today. Nobody takes the time to look at how they have gotten on there. If you see the biographies of each one of them, what you will find is that they sacrificed everything for their ambitions. If you are sitting on the couch and think about a businessman to be fancy, you were not there for the last twenty years or so when they woke up at five 'o'clock in the morning and worked sixteen hours a day to get to this moment.

If you want to transform your life or create a beautiful one, you have got to make business as the north star. Everybody talks about having and getting the things that are not normal. You talk about making billions, riding in Rolls Royce cars, being a professional gaming company, and getting paid millions to give short speeches. It is not normal to make that happen. Thus, not putting obnoxious efforts, and not giving away everything won't make it possible for you to start a business. You will have to save every penny so as to invest the amount for turning it into a substantial passive income opportunity.

People spend money on things they can't afford just to impress others around them that they don't even care about or like. That is where ninety-nine percent of people are caught up. For running a business, you need to come out of that trap with your tools. If your city is expensive, move and shift to a cheap place. If your car payments are high, sell your car and take the bus. Why do you need an apartment that stretches you out? Why is your car so fancy? Why do you want that new pair of off-whites? Why do you want to go out with friends on the weekend?

Building something big requires immense sacrifices, and people don't want to sacrifice. Many people around you are not able to do something great just because they want those two extra bedrooms they will never use. The answer comes down to sacrificing everything.

"It is not about how much money or time you have. It is all about what you are spending your money on." – Gary Vaynerchuk

Strong Beliefs

If you are not your number one fan, you have already lost, because the market is surprisingly good at tearing you down — and not only the market but your loved ones as well. To start an innovative business, you have to have a strong and unbreakable belief. That is what inspires you to move forward when things go wrong. Beliefs are the causes of making you feel good or bad at any time. Some great leaders of the world said that when you have strong beliefs, your beliefs become your thoughts, your thoughts become your actions, your actions become your habits, your habits become your character, and the character makes you win or lose depending on what kind of beliefs you had when started at first.

It is way harder to actually have your product win with customers than to have some senior officials to write you down a paycheck every month for being a laborer. The competition of the corporate world looks exactly the same as your standpoint of looking at it. If you think you will win and put in the work, you will succeed. If you feel you can't make it up, you won't. It is the law of the universe, just like there is a law of gravity. You will always get the results based on your beliefs. Think about Steve Jobs. Did he ever waste his time thinking he would not be able to do it? Not at all. In today's world, no company can even think about defeating Apple Inc.

Steve would never be able to build the company if he did not believe in himself. Believing in what you do will make it believe to the customer that you are the best.

Therefore, changing the way you look at things will change the things around you. Go out there, hit the chest, and show everyone that you are the best. You will be considered so.

"People who are crazy enough to think they can change the world are the ones who do." – Steve Jobs

Hard Work

Creating an innovative, different, and big thing requires the work. When you have the audacity to become an entrepreneur, run your businesses, and want all the riches and great things that come with it, you need to put in the work. Hard work is the first, second, and third part of the formula. If you are an employee and look at your eight hours a day, two to three of your eight hours are being spent on dumb things.

If you think you are talented enough and don't need to work much, that is a humongous mistake. The reason being is that someone hungrier to reach the top, will work harder, fight for the legacy, and reach the top before you. Talent can be a blessing, but it can also be a curse at the same time — nobody among us knowns a single person that became successful without the work. The world is full of talented individuals who never made it. The world is full of expensively educated kids that are outperformed by high school dropouts.

Talent won't get you anywhere if you don't work for it. Talent is nothing if you have no heart and guts.

The uphill-climbing work trumps everything. You can debate talent. You can debate luck, you can debate circumstances, but you can't debate if someone is cutting the teeth, grinding, and putting in the work.

Hard work always wins. Maybe not immediately, but in the end, it makes a significant difference. In the end, it changes everything. It pays forever. Hard work never lies; your dream never dies. It all comes down to you either doing it or not doing it.

But hard work doesn't mean doing a lot of physical work. It has got to be analytical and mental and should involve experiments and zeal to find better options for better results.

Hard work also involves smart work and visualization. For contextualizing explanation, let us look at a study by Dr. Biasiotto at the University of Chicago, where he split three groups and tested each one of them on how many free throws they could make with the basketball.

The first group practiced hard to make free throws for an hour every day for the next 30 days.

The second group just sat and visualized themselves, making free throws.

The third group did nothing.

After 30 days, when he tested the performance of the groups, the results were quite unexpectable and impressive.

The first group improved by 24% by practicing for an hour every day.

The second group improved the performance by 23% just from visualizing!

And as expected, the third group didn't improve at all.

This experiment explains that when you add hard work and visualization both, your chances of becoming successful or specifically, building a significant business increase to 47%. That is a point not to ignore.

"Success isn't always about greatness. It's about consistency. Consistent hard work leads to success. Greatness will come." – Dwayne Johnson

"Some people dream of success, while others wake up and work hard at it." – Napoleon Hill

Failure Tolerance

Too many people just want it to be green all the time. That doesn't happen in business. It is the same as playing outside. Sometimes it is going to be cloudy, sometimes sunny, and sometimes chilly. But if you love playing, you will do it in any of these conditions. While doing business, there could be a bunch of failures. Sometimes they are going to be micro; other times, they are going to be macro. You will have to deal with them and overcome them. Failing is the part of the equation, and you have to embrace/tolerate it. And the way you do it is by lining up things into the right and positive perspective. People, as a society, lack perspective.

Think if you lose all of your favorite people or loved ones in your family on the same day. Would getting that one new sale even matter to you at that time? No, it is not possible. That is what you should do with failures. The exciting part is that you, as a person, don't even care about your failures when researched deeply. Failures are considered inappropriate by you just because of other people's judgments.

You have grown in an environment where success is overrated, and failures are uncomfortably underrated. But in reality, both of them are complementary. The only way you overcome and tolerate failures is by not letting other voices get inside your head and deprive your beautiful path of adventures. Every successful entrepreneur/businessperson had been through gigantic failures in the past and still face them.

So, when you fail, you need to think of the alternative solution, retain yourself as quick as possible, and reverse-engineer your strategies and plans. That is how you figure stuff out and get things done at scale. How can you know the taste of berries if you don't go and taste them? When you are the only one to try new fruits, you have got to taste them all out, and hopefully, they are not poisonous. Even if they are, you can have the medicines to restore and hold yourself. What is indirectly meant by this is that every failure teaches you something, and allows you to find the best alternative solution to make you stand out. That is the core principle of business.

"Would you like me to give you a formula for success? It's quite simple, really: Double your rate of failure. You are thinking of failure as the enemy of success. But it isn't at all. You can be discouraged by failure, or you can learn from it, so go ahead and make mistakes. Make all you can. Because

remember that's where you will find success." – Thomas J. Watson

Patience

Do you have a better relationship with time? If the answer is yes, then nobody has the courage to drag you down because people generally don't. Patience plays a crucial role in a business's success. No big thing happens overnight, and the ones that do are not sustainable. A lot of passionate people in this world of billions have everything what it takes to run a business but lack patience. Before something great happens, it takes time.

The mighty time is your best friend, but it can also be your worst enemy. That depends on your ideology and lookouts.

These lines seem so impractical and theoretical, but they matter more than anything in life/business. It is equally pushing it hard, as it is patience. If you push those two extremes, you make it up. But everybody is on the one extreme or the other, and people who push both extremes win. That is why there are so few people that win. Impatience comes into business in most of the cases because a businessperson has to prove a lot of people wrong, and this feeling or excitement of proving someone wrong takes away the whole moment within one go.

Don't think about it to grow fast because it is always short-term. You have got to love the process more than the profit. You have got to enjoy the game more than the golden trophy. You have got to love the journey and route more than the destination. That is how you grow as a business. You won't be seeing sales or customers right away. It will take some long. But never forget, slow and steady wins the race. It took you twenty years or so to become self-aware and complete the random education. If you talk about months in the life of years, think before you speak. How about changing the conversation around time? How about working on and on for five years to see some impacting results? How about starting at twenty and working till thirty to live the next sixty freely? In a nutshell, you have to reconsider your expectations about time.

"A wise man does not try to hurry history. Many wars have been avoided by patience, and many have been

precipitated by reckless haste." – Adlai Stevenson

Team Work

If you don't do the necessary teamwork, either you get overloaded in the end, or your team becomes dependent on you for every task. This situation can be very pressurizing and lead to a lot of complications. Looking into other well-known industries, some of the world's most successful individuals support and believe in teamwork. As they say, it is difficult for one person to break a bundle of four wooden sticks, but it is easier for four people to do so. That is what a business is all about. What you officially call the team in the corporate world is 'staff.' It is one and the same thing. As a top executive, you will have to manage the team by helping each other, learning, and making them learn. You can't be too much careless, and you can't be too careful at the same time. Something that you are very good at should be told to the team, and something that you are not very good at should be asked to team for trying. Perfect chemistry with your team is highly required for getting at the peak of your business. If you support and work for them, they will also care and work towards your success. It is as same as the laws that the teachers had taught you. The only difference is that you don't have to be a scientist to practice this one.

"If you want to go fast, go alone. If you want to go far, go together." – African Proverb

Execution

Did you know that less than one percent of the people in this world are earning over ninety-six percent of the wealth? What it tells you is that there are less than one percent people in the world who actually execute and turn their dreams into reality. Others come to events, watch videos, read books, make themselves feel good, get inspired, and never take the required actions for the transformation. Being a practitioner always wins the game. You might be thinking that there is a lot of competition in the business/corporate world of today. But fortunately, that is not true if you choose the legacy and not focus very much on short-term gains. It is not about avoiding short-term revenues, but it is about not valuing them much. Initially and ideally, a company/business has to focus on short-term revenues; otherwise, it may collapse and die. The first year's goal should be to raise as much money as you can to experiment and spend for the end consumers' luxury in the future.

The founder and chief executive officer of Tesla company disclosed that he initially laser-focused on generating revenue and then went on creating revolutionary products.

So, the most pivotal part of the game is executing, and it is easier said than done. Execution is where ninety-nine percent of the people give up. The market doesn't care if you have the best idea and strategies unless executed. It could happen that your plans might not be efficiently implemented when practiced. Execution is the key.

And understanding execution is quite simple - people are virtually confused. They don't know what they want. They want ten thousand things. Stop being confused - decide your thing, go ahead and do it. If it works out, that is great. If it doesn't, adjust.

Just wake up, research, come up with ideas, and make it happen in real life. People don't care how much you know until they know whether or not you have done it practically. Executing helps you lead by example, and that is when you get to meet real profit, awareness, respect, and reputation.

Either you put in the heart, body, and soul to build that statue, or you don't. Starting an enterprise is binary, which means, either you lose, or you win. But if you fall in love with losing and execute on new ideas now and then, that is where the fun begins. That is where success knocks the door excitedly. In more than simple words, either you become all the way white or all the way black. Most of the people are grey/confused. After all, we know that actions speak louder than words.

"Ideas don't make you rich. The correct execution of ideas does." – Felix Dennis

Action Plan

Everything that you do without a plan will someway cost you something. Business already means something unorganized, but still, you have to create a plan or so-called 'a system' to get things flowing at the right speed and in the right direction. Having a system makes it easier to inspect the losses and gains that inspire you to create something even better than the previous one. An action plan helps you give more freedom of time which you can utilize in other vital parts like the family and all. It is not like that the plan you make will always work according to your wish. Some of the things will go against your ideas, but that is fine. When we talk about the plan, it doesn't have to be very clean, with every minor step to be followed. Instead, it can have the list and timings of relevant micro and macro events that can affect your business in scaling. The plan doesn't necessarily have to be made and designed by an expert. You, as a starter, can make it possible through your construction tools.

Having an ideal plan can also help you in the future as a resource when things go very wrong. No matter how expert you are in your field, there are moments when the mind goes blank. That is when you can look at the action plan, and it can be really handy. Ideally, an action plan comprises of various big campaigns and their subsets. It also has an alternative plan with the original one. For example, a shoe company has a simple action plan for designing, creation, check-up, and distribution. But in a case when the check-up part leads to delay, another alternative plan could be executed to divert the consumers' attention from their pre-bookings for a time to come up with the distribution efficiently so that it won't lead to a bad consumer experience or consumer inconvenience.

Now, this was just a simple instance. An advanced plan can always assist in the turns and can change the game. It can also tell you how to be financially viable.

"A goal without a plan is just a wish." – Antoine de Saint-Exupery

Innovative Product/Service

You want to build a business or become an entrepreneur because you want to be rich and make more money. But people are not going to give you money because you want to be wealthy. They are going to pay for solutions to their problems that they expect from your products or services. The punchline is this; if you want to build a winning business, you want to have winning products. Your products have to solve the problems of the people.

When Amazon's Kindle platform started, it was a completely different concept back in 2007. People had to visit tens of bookstores in the hope of getting their desired book before the Kindle platform went live. It was one of the most innovative products which reduced people's stress of visiting several different shops for no good reason and just to buy a book. For it helped not only the readers save their time, but also the environmental problems of cutting trees for paper, there are millions of people using it every single day presently. Times have evolved. People have gotten smarter and intellectual. You can't trick them and should not with the same thing by tweaking it a little bit.

For creating an innovative product, you need to look at the present market scenario. Which products are selling the most in your industry? How are they helping customers? How satisfied are the buyers? What are the prices? How is the design? How are the products helping the environment?

The list goes on and on. Basically, you need to go through every aspect and then decide to create a better yet cost-effective thing that promotes ease. It is going to take an incredibly long time and work if you are thinking about building a deluxe business with high-ticket products like Gucci and Armani.

To raise the capital for making costly/profitable/popular products, primarily, you will need to sell premium products at non-premium prices.

"Don't find customers for your products. Find products for your customers." – *Seth Godin*

Courage To Bear The Tall Poppy Syndrome

This is the world where both positivity and negativity reside. There are good feelings, and there are bad feelings. They are present everywhere around you. Especially in the corporate world, negativity has been overrated. So, when you start an innovative business model or business in general, there will be a majority of people who won't like to see you succeed. You will be exposed to strange scenes where your competitors will try to cut your throat and throw you away by increasing the volume of the cons of your business, but if you have the courage to bear that all, it will be an easy way for you in the eventuality.

The tall poppy syndrome is a culture in the corporate world where the one with high status is attacked, resented, criticized, and cut down by the ones who are not. When you are the tall poppy, everyone is going to bring you down, and when you are not, you will be influenced to bring other poppies down by your companions. But you don't have to worry about it (just have to ignore it).

There are two ways to build the biggest building in the town. One is, just be good enough to build the biggest building in the town. Two, try to tear down everybody else's buildings. But there is also the fact that people who try to tear down other people's buildings have always been disrespected.

Hence, going well with the option of being better than others and not caring about the culture will lead to greatness.

"If people are trying to bring you down, it only means that you are above them." – Amy Rees Anderson

Hiring And Firing

Sure, team caring and work is super important. But the process of building involves great things like hiring and not so great as hiring, and you will have to get through it. You will have to move forward, disregarding the emotions. When you are hiring somebody for the first time, most of the time, they are the known ones who are hired because those are the people whom you trust. But when you get to see that they are not doing anything good for the business and are rather just taking advantage of being a relative, you will have to fire them. This is the feeling which the majority of the people are not good at. The truth is, things happen in life, and you have to take appropriate and desired actions to build something big.

Another big problem in this process of team recruiting is the ego. Everybody thinks he is super smart to examine people's potential and can hire the right people. But when you hire somebody and he is not the right person for your organization, it is difficult for you to fire them easily. Why? Because this proves you and your beliefs wrong that you are good at hiring. Thus, disregarding the ego, it is good to accept the truth and learn how to fire people fast. That is how you build the team of your dreams.

Also, hiring should not be done based on educational documents, for they are just irrelevant. Everybody can bubble up multiple-choice questions and pursue high-level degrees. That doesn't define how good and creative the person is. Some of the biggest companies in the world like Google, Apple, Netflix, IBM, and Starbucks, don't require any college degrees for hiring. Because what they are looking for is creative, skillful, and passionate human beings instead of slaves. The best way you can hire somebody is by providing some kind of position-related task and then ask the aspirant to accomplish it in front of you or the team. Or a round table discussion with industry experts is the best way to know someone's potential.

You don't have to overthink it. It is just a process of getting wrong things right and nothing rocket-science. Luckily, nobody is good at hiring. You have got to get good at firing.

"Hiring is guessing, firing is not." – Gary Vaynerchuk

Adaption To Changes

Those times of traditional billboards and yellow pages have come to an end. The world is not as easy as it used to be in the past times. There have been a lot of changes taking place. The fittest business is the one that accepts changes and adapts accordingly. If BMW had stuck to the old vintage models of cars and not accept the evolution of technology, they wouldn't have even existed presently. Business is not about being conservative. It is the game of what is next and what is better. You have no idea if Nike would come out with a concept of a new energy drink and outsource the Boost energy drink by Nestlé. Audi could come out with a new headphone with a beautiful logo presenting the four rings to outperform JBL. You must have come across many of these kinds of changes already.

Technology matters. It always wins as it is always there to provide better solutions to the users. You can't think of being stable in a world that constantly moves. People and the market don't give a second to you if you don't meet their requirements and expectations.

Other people are trying really hard to make a better and efficient thing than yours. The market has so many different alternatives that people don't bother to look at you.

Taking the responsibility of being a leader, making a cultural shift, and being creative will open the doors of further growth. There is a need to structure the team to maximize its potential, set challenging, achievable, and engaging targets, resolve conflicts quickly and effectively, show passion, believe in the future vision, be persuasive, empower innovation, and last but not the least, remain positive and supportive.

You will need to change the conversation about what got you at the top. This will give your business a chance to stand out in the existing competition and market. Even if you are raising capital to sell it, it has to be sustainable, and for that, adjusting to the changes is a must.

"By changing nothing, nothing changes." – Tony Robbins

*Quick tip – <u>Please don't build a financial arbitrage machine, build a sustainable business. If you are building it to sell, you have already lost.</u>

How To Scale A Business?

Once you have an up and running business (either online or offline), the next thing you think about is scaling it. But before going after scaling, you need to think of whether scaling it is profitable in the execution or not. Never forget that bigger is not always better. Not every business is meant to scale, and scaling for the sake of it can be a huge mistake.

For example, if you have a business of jackets with a valuation of ten million dollars and you want to scale it to a hundred million, you need to consider if that is going to be profitable/sustainable or not. If your expenses and funds purely depend on sales, you have got to slow it down and not think of scaling as that will lead to constant financial pressure and struggles.

Then, you will either have to raise capital and scale it from there or change your business model. The model has to be smart to get the most out off of the scaling process. Let us see how to scale an already surviving business.

Collaboration

Collaboration is one of the most outspoken and powerful strategies that can be used to scale a business to the next level. There are many big and small businesses/companies seeking collaboration for increasing awareness and growth. The question is – how exactly collaboration can help you?

Collaborating with others will inspire you to look for other cost-effective and smooth ways to get things done fast. When you are alone, there is only one core strategy or system, but with a partnership, you get to see other new tools, methods, and procedures. This will unleash new ideas within you that can speed up the process of scaling. Collaboration also helps in the expansion of your network. Whether as an individual or a business, but it will assist in connecting with a newer audience, which can help you understand more about consumers' behavior and requirements.

As collaborating with other businesses or businesspersons gives you extra hands-on work, reduce expenses, and reduce costs, this way, you will end up saving a lot of money which would be spent for no good.

"Coming together is a beginning, staying together is progress, and working together is success." – Henry Ford

Provide Free Value Forever

Do you know the best secret to grow a business at scale? It is providing free value forever. That is true. Unfortunately, most of the shops are caught up in the company culture of considering profit as the bottom line. The hard truth is that most of the businesses you see, crushing it today, will not be able to do so in the near future of technology. Anything based on hooking people and then pressurizing them to turn into customers is the worst strategy of all times. Just look at the top businesses or companies of this planet. What do they do? They are providing as much free value as they can to the end consumer. The ones who are not doing this have already started to decline and will continue to go down the black path. Just to give you some context, think about the free rides that Uber gives to people, the free deliveries Amazon gives to the purchasers, and the free consulting big agencies are giving. Why do you think they are doing this? The reason is that providing free value had, has, and will have the most leverage.

People trust you more than anything when you keep the free value upfront.

People think most of the money is made on the frontend, but the reality is, the highest amounts of money are always made on the backend. You should consider the lifetime value of a customer instead of chasing a one-time payment. Once you build that trust with your customers, you get exposed to their known ones and keep getting more and more highly interested userbase overtime.

Some great businesspeople said that if you spend a dollar on a customer and make fifty cents, you are smart business. That is what you should be doing. Get out of the rate race of chasing Return On Investment (ROI), provide free value without worrying about the short-term matrices, give some time for your business to take a breath, and then scale it exponentially well with the customer referrals.

*"Providing free value at scale is the best strategy to get customers at scale." –
Shivansh Bhanwariya*

Care For Your Customers

How do you feel about the person who takes care of you and respect everything you say and do? For sure, it is going to feel good. That is what happens with customers of a particular business. No matter how good you are at your services, how good your products are, and how good your knowledge base is, but if you don't take care of your customers, it is done for.

It is because people don't care how much you know until they know how much you care. So, you genuinely need to care for the people who come in to know more about your business and decide to be a part of it instead of showing that you care a lot for them.

When you look at the goals of companies like Google and LinkedIn, they are super focused on their customer experience. If you don't like something and report to the executives, they feel sorry about it and try to help you out without any expectations. That is how they own hundreds of millions of people who are ready to spend tons of money on them. It is not only the way for big companies to grow; it is also applicable to small and medium-sized businesses.

When you go so much above and beyond for the users, they fall in love with you. They like and celebrate it when your business becomes successful just because you care.

Let's say you have a restaurant business, if a customer comes in for the first time and you take amazing care, the statistical likelihood of them doing the second visit is about forty percent. When they visit you the second time and perceives amazing flawless experience, the statistical likelihood of them doing the third visit is still about forty-two percent. The third time they come, and you care fantastically well, the statistical likelihood of them doing the fourth visit is over seventy percent. Once they come in the fourth time, you own them. That is when you do the scaling. The conclusion is this; you have to care very much for your people before they turn into supportive lifetime customers. When your customers want you to grow, you build a meaningful business.

In consequence, if you want to grow and scale your business to the peak, you need to do it with the heart, not the brain, because most people think customers as robots and treat them as credit cards. Always look for opportunities on how you can help your customers and bring them value.

"There is only one boss. The customer – and he can fire everybody in the company from the chairman on down, simply by spending his money somewhere else." – Sam Walton

Show Up To Customers

Whether the business is physically based or online, showing up to customers can give an impacting push to your growth. People are not fools. They understand it when you connect to them with the help of a bot when online. They do know that they are talking to a sneaky salesperson when they are offline on a call. You need to show up to them for building better relationships. When you make that deep relationship, they are much more likely to contribute to the company's success. There is not a whole bunch of processes involved in it. You just need to have somebody that can connect physically, listens to the consumer's problem, try to bring them the best possible solution at the lowest reasonable price when it is a physical business.

On the other hand, if it is an online business, you necessitate to show up live and answer people's questions one-on-one. Everybody knows that you run those pre-recorded webinars to drive more sales. But doing that doesn't satisfy the customers. You don't necessarily have to appear in front of the customer every time, but some most knowledgeable and interactive people in your team can make it happen.

This is going to generate more revenue, get your word out to more people, increase the authority of your business, and fuel it for reaching the sky.

"Spend a lot of time talking to customers face-to-face. You would be amazed at how many companies don't listen to their customers." – H. Ross Perot

Chase The Attention

As mentioned earlier, the attention of the consumers has to totally changed. No one pays attention to your worthless billboards, which cost thousands of dollars. No one likes to watch the nasty television commercial you bought for millions. There is no point in wasting your money on the useless yellow pages that don't mean a penny to your business. The attention of the end consumer has completely transformed in the new era of technology. In the yore, people sat with their families and watched their favorite shows on the television. That doesn't happen now. People are more comfortable spending time on platforms like Netflix, Amazon Prime, YouTube, Instagram, Facebook, LinkedIn, and lots more. They are the mobile phones where people like to consume content at present. You need to take it into your account. Right now, the price to get your business in front of consumers is so underpriced that this is the greatest era in the whole history, to ever be alive and be an entrepreneur or own your own business if you want it to happen. You can literally pull out your mobile device, open camera, record an inspiring sales video, and get it live in front of thousands, hundreds of thousands, or even millions of highly targeted customers, and scale your business at the fastest speed possible through the internet. The internet is just a few years old, and it allows playing the whole game for free. It doesn't care whether you are big or small, African or American, white or black, and successful or unsuccessful. If you make the best content for people and impress them to buy, you will win, disregarding Microsoft being your competition.

You can show up in front of the relevant people without hurting their flow of consuming something and grab their attention. Attention is the fundamental asset for a business to grow. It keeps changing. On the internet itself, it was the blogs, now it is video, and in the coming future, it is going to be the voice. But once you know what people are spending most of their time on, and adjust your mechanism accordingly, you win every time.

These channels, like social media, content platforms, and search engines, just provide you the medium. The rest of it depends on your creativity. For some context, if you run advertisements in the United States, there should be American people in your ads, whereas if you run advertisements in Africa, there should be African people in the ads instead of Americans for there will be more chances of a native person seeing a native presentation. This is the process of understanding the attention.

Believe it or not, but if you are very much passionate about finding the best scaling opportunity, utilizing the internet to catch the attention of the buyers is the best thing you could possibly do instead of chasing traditional methods. It is so underpriced, which makes it the best customer acquisition channel ever at present. Bill Gates says that if your business is not on the internet, you will be out of business shortly. That is true, as he has been historically correct for the last couple of decades or so. It is already proven.

"Your business lives in the room where your ideal customers like to live." – Shivansh Bhanwariya

Change The Intent

The success of you and your business is predicated on the intent. The intent of you giving free information, the intention behind cold or warm calling, the intention of sending emails and messages, or something else, has to be to help the customers meet their needs. So many people believe that empathy and kindness are the weaknesses in society. They deem that if you try to help somebody with something, almost every time they don't accept it or simply take the advantage. People assume that the nice times have been over. Honestly, those are misleading beliefs. It is because the people who help presently have a selfish intent behind giving. Giving with expecting something in return is not giving. There were people in the past who tried to help customers and won, and there are people who have built huge empires just by being empathetic or what the present society calls girly or motherly. If you really care about that one customer and try to help, this might be weird, but the law of attraction takes place here. By doing this, more similar people are going to be presented in front of you whom your business call as potential customers. This is not just a theory or thesis but a practical reality. The conclusion is simple; kindness is the ultimate strength in our society. When you give them with a positive intention, they give it back to your business naturally.

"If your organization's intentions transcend the mere act of selling a product or service, and it is brave

enough to expose its heart and soul, people will respond. They will connect. They will like you. They will talk. They will buy." – Gary Vaynerchuk

Winning Marketing

Business needs a killer marketing to stand out. The more successful your marketing campaigns are, the better off you are going to be. Having a great product, caring for people, providing excellent customer service, and committing to your values is perfect. The real challenge is winning the market. And the way you do it is with winning marketing.

You need to promote the business is the most impressive and cost-efficient way possible in the options. For marketing a business smartly, you don't need the Kardashians to promote your products and services. They don't bring in the return on your investments.

The top-performing marketing type is digital marketing. It is the promotion of your business through all of the digital media that your potential customers are currently using - whether those are mobile phones, computers, tablets, radios, or anything else.

Expected results could be generated through this strategy when a skillful digital marketing executive gets the work done for you. It involves both online and offline marketing.

Calling people to promote your products is an example of offline digital marketing and showing them advertisements on Facebook or

YouTube is an example of online digital marketing.

The good news is that they both are beneficial if implemented correctly, keeping in mind the 'rule of seven.' The 'rule of seven' is a marketing rule which claims that you need to show up or connect at least seven times with a customer before they decide to buy something and contribute to your business. The most appropriate reason for this rule is trust. It takes time for the customer to determine whether you are trustworthy or not, and when they see you over and over again, you become familiar and win their trust.

As the world is getting attracted to the web more and more, it is imperative to look at the choices in online marketing as well. Online marketing involves seven types of marketing channels.

It starts with Search Engine Optimization (SEO), where you promote your business by creating content for your target audience and get it live on search engines like Google, Bing, and Yahoo. Then there is Search Engine Marketing (SEM) where you advertise on search engines like Google and Bing to get customers. After that, there is Social Media Marketing (SMM) where you promote by creating social-friendly content. Then it is Content Marketing where you reach out to successful businesses within your industry for marketing your content and brand. Next, there is Paid Advertising on all popular platforms from the Forbes website to Facebook ads. It is the Email Marketing where promotion takes place via emails. And at last, there is Affiliate Marketing where you find other people to promote your services and products.

When you combine all of these channels and show some consistency, you will notice that your business will grow at the fastest speed you would have ever imagined. Top companies in the world have already started taking advantage of digital marketing, and now, it is time for you. Other strategies to leverage in marketing are brand storytelling, hosting events, and going to events. Storytelling is a very underrated strategy. If you can tell a true and engaging story, customers get excited to help your business grow. Why? It is because people buy emotions, not things. Some great marketers like Gary Vaynerchuk, Neil Patel, Rand Fishkin, and Larry Kim believe that true marketing is all about telling your story truly. Also, storytelling is one of the best ways to build an evergreen brand. Once you build a brand, you have the solutions to every problem.

But always remember – marketing is not just about campaigns; it is about connections, content, commitments, and conversations.

"Whether B2B or B2C, I believe passionately that good marketing essentials are the same. We all are emotional beings looking for relevance, context, and connection." – Beth Comstock

"Good marketing makes the company look smart. Great marketing makes the customer feel smart." – Joe Chernov

"Content is king." – Bill Gates

*Quick tip – <u>If you have an online business, try to have it running 24 hours a day as that will lead to fast and consistent results.</u>

Speed Up The Process

You have been taught to be in the prison of perfection since your childhood - the punishment for making mistakes, for experimenting, for trying new things, talking with strangers, and whatnot. In business, that doesn't matter. The market moves with speed of light, and people forget you within seconds. If you don't move with the speed of the market, it will be harder for you to survive. Nothing is perfect, and nothing should be so. Speed is a billion times more important than perfection. The amount of you that are crippled by getting things right instead of getting things done is completely insane.

So, if you want to scale fast, you have got to speed up the process. For doing this, you will require more team members, tools, strategists, marketers, and ideas. It doesn't matter if you get two things wrong and twenty things right. The majority always wins. Make rules that your staff has to follow and set daily targets to complete at any cost. Come to practicing instead of having long five-hour business meetings as doing is always better than thinking or discussing.

When you have two binary options, don't waste your time in overthinking. Whichever one you choose, you will never ever have an idea of how the other one would have played out. Just go about doing it fast, and when you increase your speed, it will be easier for you to scale faster.

"If everything seems under control, you're not going fast enough." — Mario Andretti

Disrupt The Industry

The most powerful step you can take to grow your business at a faster rate is disrupting the current industry; in other words, doing just opposite to what your competitors are doing. If your competitors are not providing free customer services to people who are not their customers, you go about doing that. If your competitors are charging a hundred dollars for something that is manufactured for fifty-dollars, you go about charging seventy dollars.

As a person who wants to generate as much revenue as possible, you must be wondering that it is not a good decision. But as you know that only one percent of the people are actually making money, people for sure will like cheaper items with the same quality. By the numbers, if you have a hundred customers for a hundred dollars, you make ten-thousand dollars on that, and if you have two hundred customers for seventy, you make fourteen-thousands dollars. That is how you grow fast if the quality is kept in mind at the same time.

This is called disruption. There are four things necessary for disrupting an industry – conviction, competing, contribution, and challenging conventional thinking.

Conviction refers to having so much love towards the industry that you are in.

Competing refers to whether or not your product has the ability to compete with the current marketplace.

Contribution means you should have the zeal to contribute to people's lives and the market.

Challenging conventional thinking means you have got to have solid thinking that challenges all the big and small competitors. If you are involved in an industry, and you don't challenge everybody's way of thinking where people are dying for you to go out of business, you are not really disrupted. You have to differentiate yourself from others for better results.

"The reason why it is so difficult for existing firms to capitalize on disruptive innovations is that their processes and their business model that make them good at the existing business actually make them bad at competing for the disruption." – Clayton Christensen

How To Manage A Scaling Business?

It is not just about scaling it. It is also about managing it for the better. There is a lot of pain and stress while managing a tremendously growing business. Let us look at some ways you can implement to manage a scaling business.

Treat Your Employees

People working for you play a critical role in the company's growth. There are people that go so much above and beyond and work ridiculously hard to grow your business. Those people should not be ignored. What you can do is have some events where people are motivated and rewarded for their efforts every month. Or you could keep special perks if an employee completes his/her targets in record time. Some certifications could also be given that can help employees in their future, and the list goes as long as you think.

The basic conclusion is that you need to take care of the people working for you, praise them, and help them in every situation like giving them free time for their families, granting leaves, supporting their ambitions, and minimizing the work pressure. This will lead them to be more loyal to the company, which will result in not only a healthy and innovative business environment but also a massive growth of your organization.

According to research by Gallup, 75 percent of the workers who voluntarily left their job did so because of their bosses and not the position itself. So, as you bring value to the end consumer, you should also do it for your staff for people don't quit jobs, they quit bosses.

"Treat your employees to the right, so that they don't use your internet to search for a new job." – Mark Zuckerberg

Control Your Expenses

One thing for you as a businessperson or an entrepreneur should be obvious – business is all about bringing the money in, not taking the money out. A scary thing in today's world of business being cool is that people tend to forget that building a sustainable business takes new investments and capital every single day. If you are buying the apartment of your dreams or the cars of your dreams, you need to check whether it will have an effect on your business in the upcoming time. If so, avoid making such decisions because when you do that, your business will start feeling like a job instead of being fun.

You may go under stress, and the organization can start to collapse faster than it was growing. Just for example, if you make a million dollars a month, you have to put that amount back into the business rather than buying a Bentley or a Lamborghini. Those are secondary things.

You must be thinking that you want that fancy car or that elegant house for the content. But that is not for satisfaction; it is for your insecurity. When you have that money sitting in the bank account, you can do something about it to find new growth opportunities. That is how big business should be managed.

Find Partners and Enable Crowdfunding

To low down the work pressure, finding partners and co-owners will reduce the overall pain. Managing a growing company won't give you much time to spend with your family. Business is important, but not more than your family. For getting more time, you can find other eligible people to partner and manage the working model. You will be shocked to know that your partners or co-founders are going to work harder than you to manage the business. It sometimes happens that you feel it so hard to tackle the growth or the customer base. At this time, your co-owners or partners can help you manage things smoothly. Also, you can enable crowdfunding where other large numbers of interested people could be found who will add small amounts of money to raise capital gradually. Crowdfunding can help your business in the validation process when a product is launched. At last, it can also help your business get more exposure, so you don't need to work overtime to find more ways to bring awareness.

An Advice To Sustain A Business

You have finally covered all the important things that are necessary to build, scale, and manage a business. It

.

is time to learn the last and one of the most undervalued strategies to sustain a business lifelong. Are you ready for this? It is building a community.

The beautiful world of the internet gives you a powerful weapon that you can utilize for your goods, which is, it allows you to build communities. Great brands like Samsung, Apple, Coca-cola, Toyota, Microsoft, Google, McDonald's, Amazon, Disney, and more have already built successful communities where people can share their views, access the brand support, and do pretty much everything to make their life better. If you as a business also utilize this strategy, what you will find is the more people (customers) are going to be attracted to you slowly and slowly.

For building a community, you need to define your business goals, find your target audience, find the best ways to connect with your community, focus on community-specific products and content, show consistency towards building awareness, constantly give back to customers and make them happy by solving their problems, ask for feedback and do surveys, organize contests, and develop a value-driven presence on all major social media sites or platforms.

This will empower your growth very widely. Maybe not immediately, but in the long run, you will outsource everyone within your industry just by having a loyal and professional community that will be interested in buying from you.

"Selling to people who actually want to hear from you is more effective than

interrupting strangers that don't." -
Seth Godin

A BOOK

BY SHIVANSH BHANWARIYA